THE LONGEST RIVERS LEAD TO THE BIGGEST OCEANS

GEOGRAPHY BOOKS FOR KIDS AGE 9-12 CHILDREN'S GEOGRAPHY BOOKS

BABY PROFESSOR

EDUCATION KIDS

Speedy Publishing LLC

40 E. Main St. #1156

Newark, DE 19711

www.speedypublishing.com

Copyright 2017

In this book, we're going to talk about the longest rivers in the world. So, let's get right to it!

WHAT IS A RIVER?

A river is essentially flowing water that comes from a natural source. There are rivers on every continent and on almost every type of land. Some rivers flow the whole year and others are seasonal, which means they flow only on wet years. A river can be a mile or less long or it may be so long that it travels through a whole continent.

THE ANATOMY OF A RIVER

Every river is different, but they all have some characteristics in common.

One thing that all rivers have in common is that they have a source. However, there are many different types of sources for rivers, such as:

- A melting glacier or glaciers
- Melting snow
- A lake that has a stream flowing from it
- A spring that flows from deep underground

A MELTING GLACIER

From its beginning source or headwaters, a river travels downhill, starting as a small stream. Its energy comes from the gravity that pulls it down toward the Earth.

The steeper its slope is, the faster it travels. If it has a very steep slope and a huge volume of water, its energy can change the shape of the land it travels.

Over time, it tears rocks and soil away from the land and over thousands or millions of years, it changes the surface of the Earth.

For example, The Grand Canyon was carved out by the erosion caused by the Colorado River.

Once a river flows from its source, rain and water from the ground add to its flow. Generally, other streams feed their water into the river as well. These "branches" of the river are known as tributaries. For example, over 1,000 tributaries feed into the mighty Amazon River. The main river plus its tributaries create a river system, which is sometimes called a watershed or drainage basin.

The river's end is called its "mouth." At this location, the river's waters empty into another waterway, such as a larger river, a natural lake, or one of the five oceans. The largest rivers on Earth generally empty into one of the oceans.

WAIMAKARIRI RIVER MOUTH

THE MOUTH OF CRAWFORDSBURN RIVER

As the river gets closer to its mouth, its currents move more slowly. It is carrying a heavy amount of sediment, and that weight means it has less energy to carve out the land.

Sometimes at its mouth, it drops off so much sediment that it creates a new landmass called a delta. Not every river has a delta.

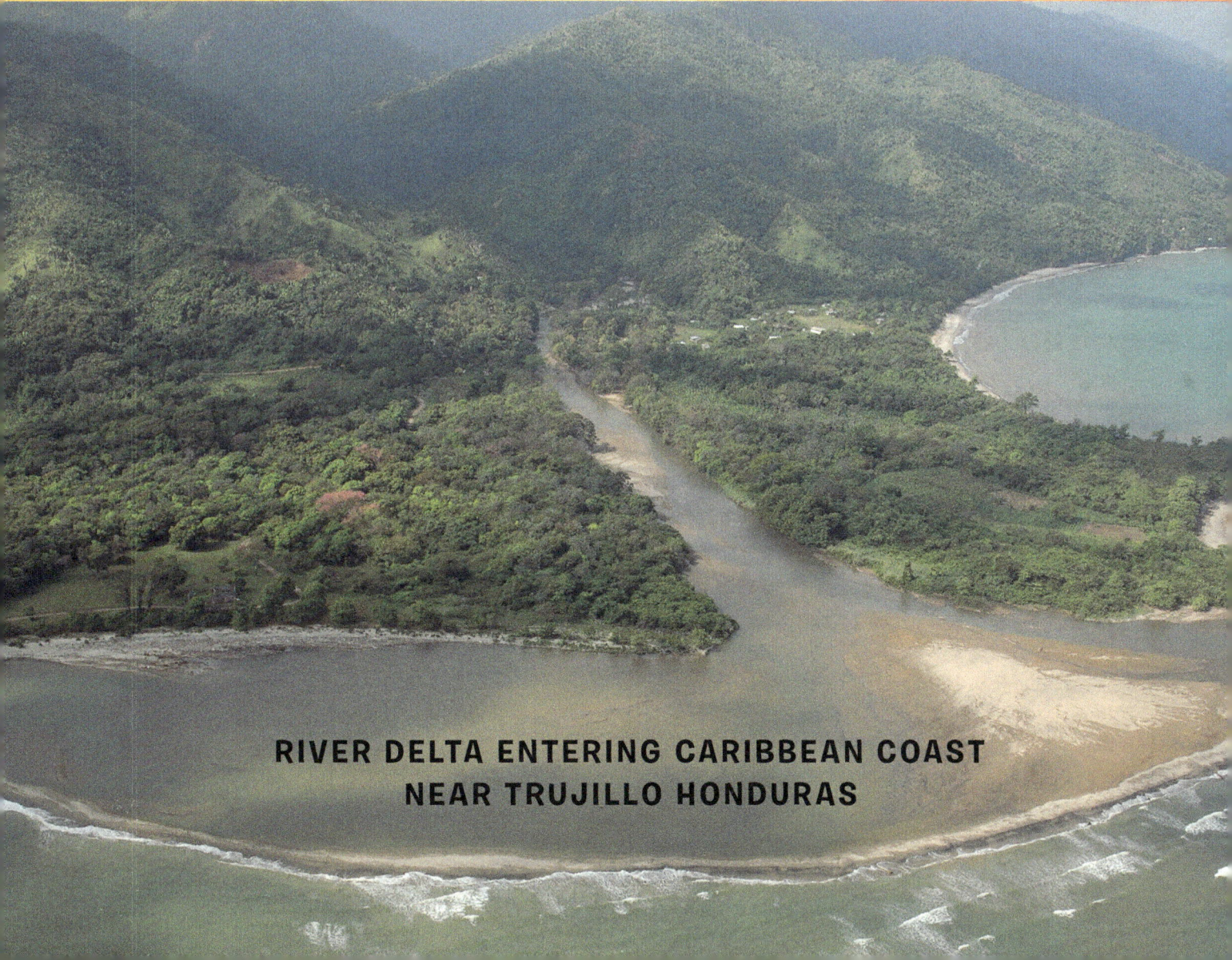

RIVER DELTA ENTERING CARIBBEAN COAST
NEAR TRUJILLO HONDURAS

For example, the Amazon empties into the Atlantic Ocean, but the currents of the ocean sweep away the sediment so no delta forms. The Nile River and the Ganges River both have very fertile deltas, which provide major farming areas for the countries of Egypt and Bangladesh, respectively.

NILE RIVER

WHY ARE RIVERS IMPORTANT?

Rivers are critical to life on Earth. They carry huge quantities of water from the surface of the land to the five oceans. The ocean's seawater is in a continuous cycle. It evaporates into the atmosphere forming clouds.

The clouds are holding tanks for moisture and they eventually release it in the form of rain, snow, sleet, freezing rain, or hail. This water, which is freshwater, helps to feed rivers as well as smaller streams. This continuous movement of water between the air, the land, and the ocean is the cycle of water. Freshwater is vital to almost all living plants and animals on Earth.

Nile river

Amazon river

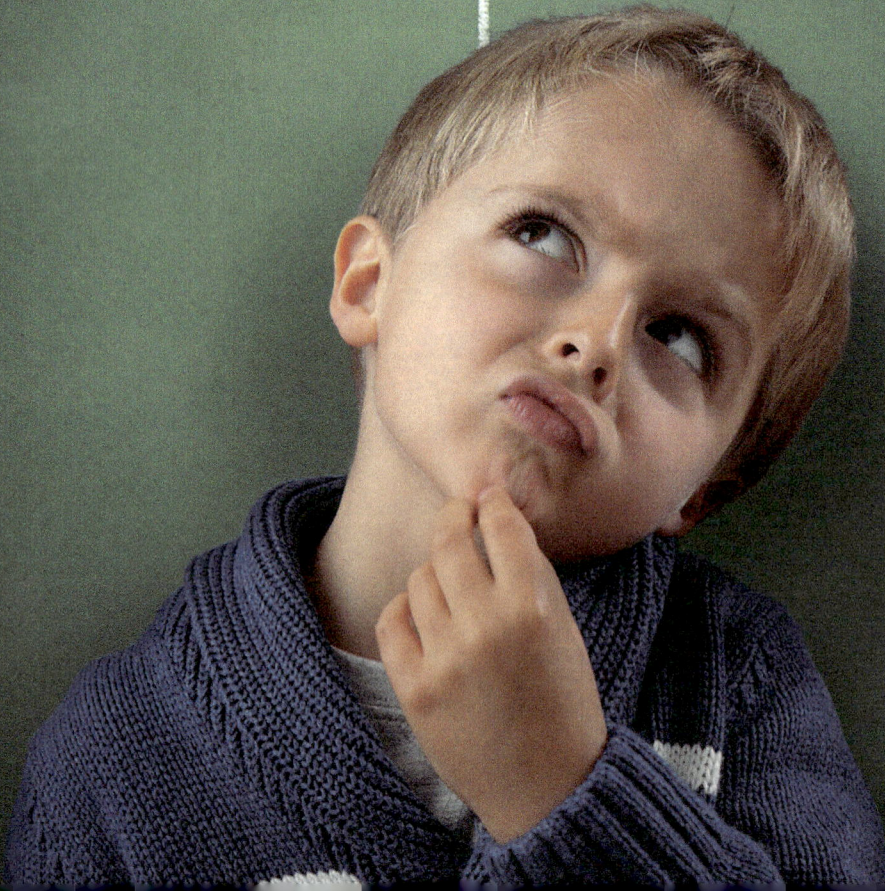

WHICH ONE IS LONGER, THE AMAZON OR THE NILE?

For centuries the debate has continued concerning whether South America's Amazon River or whether Africa's Nile River is the longest river on Earth. The truth is that rivers aren't easy to measure. It's next to impossible to pinpoint the exact location of a river's source. Also, where it ends is difficult to measure as well. The length of rivers sometimes changes too, since their deltas can get bigger or smaller.

The Amazon River is estimated to be somewhere in the range of 3,900 miles to 4,225 miles long. The Nile River is estimated to be somewhere in the range of 3,437 miles to 4,180 miles long. Since we don't know the exact distance for them, the longest river could be either one. However, there are two things we do know.

They are definitely the top two in the category of the world's longest rivers. We also know that the Amazon holds and carries more water than any of the other rivers on Earth. In fact, about 20% of all freshwater that reaches the oceans comes from the Amazon River!

NILE RIVER

THE NILE RIVER IN AFRICA

Most scientists believe that the Nile is the longest river on Earth. The source of the Nile is thought to be small streams that feed into Lake Victoria. It travels from south to north and empties into the Mediterranean Sea.

A huge delta has been formed where the Nile empties. The White Nile River, whose source is in Rwanda, and the Blue Nile River, whose source is in Ethiopia, are both tributaries of the Nile and meet

at the city of Khartoum in the country of Sudan. From there, the river travels through the lands of the Sahara Desert and then eventually ends at the Mediterranean.

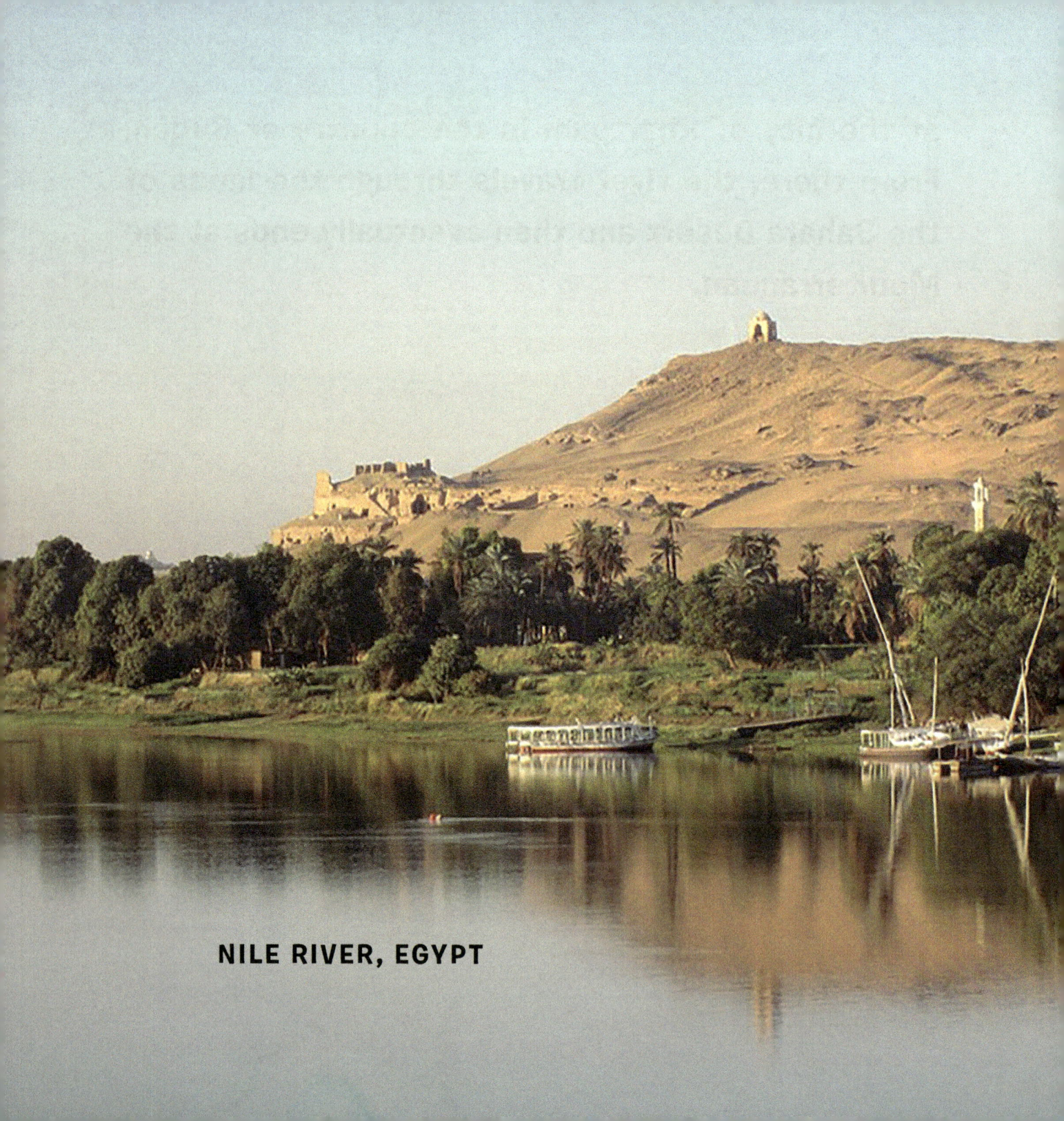

NILE RIVER, EGYPT

Most of the population of Egypt lives near the river. It's confusing on a map because the Upper Nile is further south since it's closer to the source and the Lower Nile is north and travels through Egypt. Eleven countries contain part of the Nile's basin.

THE AMAZON RIVER IN SOUTH AMERICA

Even if it's not as long as the Nile, there's no doubt that the Amazon is the mightiest river on Earth. Its strength is huge compared to all the others. If you added up the water carried by the Mississippi in the United States, the Yangtze in China, and the Nile in Africa, it still wouldn't total the amount of water carried by the Amazon.

AMAZON RIVER

The Amazon is also one of the widest rivers on Earth. At points, it measures seven miles across and during the wet season it can measure as wide as twenty-five miles across. The river's power is so great that there are no places where bridges can safely be built!

A very cold stream from the upper elevations of the Andes Mountains located in Peru is the beginning source of the Amazon. The river and its tributaries flow through six different South American countries with the longest distance in Brazil. It travels from west to east and then empties in the Atlantic Ocean at a location in northeastern Brazil.

ANDES MOUNTAINS

YANGTZE RIVER

THE YANGTZE RIVER IN CHINA

The most important as well as the longest river in Asia is the Yangtze River in China. Its headwaters are in the Dangla Mountains, which are located between the country of Tibet and the country of China in the province of Qinghai. It travels for about 3,915 miles before its mouth reaches the East China Sea where it empties.

The Yangtze has long been a water highway for trade as well as a region with abundant agriculture. Its valley is perfect for growing rice, and water from the river is used for irrigation. Many Chinese people live on the river in junks, which are houseboats.

FAMOUS BEND OF YANGTZE RIVER

THREE GORGES DAM ON THE YANGTZE RIVER

The Yangtze is home to what is currently the world's largest and most powerful plant for hydroelectric power. It's able to produce over 22,000 megawatts of power for affordable electricity. However, recently the leadership in China has become concerned by the amount of environmental damage the dam appears to be doing to the surrounding area, which is highly populated by people, animals, and plants.

THE MISSISSIPPI-MISSOURI-JEFFERSON RIVER IN NORTH AMERICA

The chief river in North America is the Mississippi River and its companion rivers the Missouri and the Jefferson. The system starts at a river called the Red Rocks River in Montana. This river becomes the Jefferson River, which combines with two other rivers to create the Missouri River.

JEFFERSON RIVER

Once the Missouri River travels the boundary dividing South Dakota from Nebraska as well as part of the boundary dividing Nebraska and Iowa, it gets to the state of Missouri.

North of the city of Saint Louis, the Missouri River flows into the mighty Mississippi.

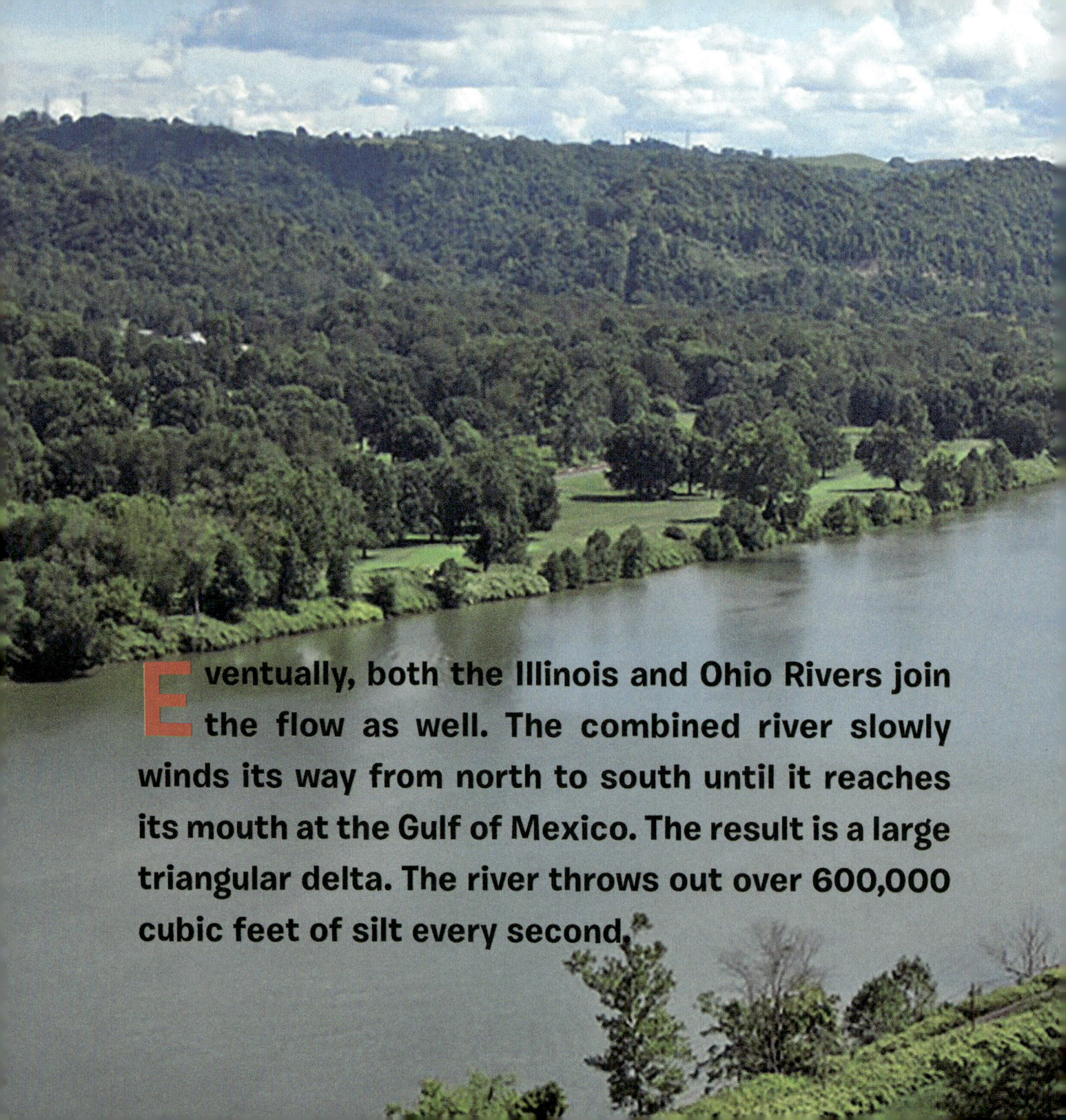

Eventually, both the Illinois and Ohio Rivers join the flow as well. The combined river slowly winds its way from north to south until it reaches its mouth at the Gulf of Mexico. The result is a large triangular delta. The river throws out over 600,000 cubic feet of silt every second.

MINNEAPOLIS-MISSISSIPPI

The three rivers, the Jefferson, the Missouri, and the Mississippi, in combination travel 3,979 miles through the heart of the United States. The river system is so big that it can be divided into seven basins created by its major tributaries.

YENISEI RIVER

OTHER NOTABLE RIVERS

YENISEI

The Yenisei has its headwaters in Mongolia. It travels 3,445 miles through Russia to its mouth at the Kara Sea, which is located in the Arctic Ocean.

YELLOW

The second longest in China and sixth longest in the world, the Yellow River travels for 3,398 miles until its mouth deposits water into the Bohai Sea.

OB-IRTYSH

The Ob and Itrysh Rivers combine to form a river system that travels 3,364 miles long as it winds it way through the countries of Russia as well as Mongolia and China to end in the Gulf of Ob.

Awesome! Now you know more about some of the longest rivers in the world. You can find more Geography books from Baby Professor by searching the website of your favorite book retailer.

Visit

BABY PROFESSOR
EDUCATION KIDS

www.BabyProfessorBooks.com
to download Free Baby Professor eBooks
and view our catalog of new and exciting
Children's Books

CPSIA information can be obtained
at www.ICGtesting.com
Printed in the USA
LVOW05s1936080118
562248LV00011B/333/P